D1531542

DATE RAPE
It's Not Your Fault

by
Joan Meijer

PUBLISHED BY:
JEM Publishing
2851 West Avenue L
Lancaster CA 93536
JoanMeijer@gmail.com

ISBN Number : 978-1499353976

Dedicated: To my sister Suzy Prudden, my support system and best friend.

Date Rape: It's Not Your Fault
Introduction

My sister, Suzy Prudden, said to me one day before she left the house for a date, "I'm a little scared, I started out with a long list of things I was never going to do and that list is getting shorter and shorter."

She was not alone, of course. Both men and women start out with sexual lists. However, while they contain many of the same things, they are very different lists. The woman's To Do List contains the things she is never going to do – or certainly not before marriage – and women give ground slowly. The man's list is a To Do list, to be worked through as fast as possible. The women's list is a compilation of what they don't want to do before marriage – or at least not right away and is the conversation that has to happen at least with themselves to avoid most date rapes. If they have this conversation they are likely to make fewer mistakes that endanger them than if they don't.

I say, "Most date rapes," because some people will commit rape with or without that conversation.

I know so many men and women who don't talk about the important things in their lives before they become problematic. I recently had a conversation with a young man about his absolute desire not to father children. At the time, he was dating a much younger woman who wanted children very badly. He told me that he had told her repeatedly that he didn't want children and he was afraid she would stop using birth control and settle the matter for him.

"If you really feel that strongly about not having children, take control of it and have a vasectomy," I suggested.

"Oh yeah, I could do that and not tell her," was his happy reply.

"You have to tell her. She has to be able to make the informed choice whether she wants to stay with you or have children."

The words, "…but she might leave me," hung between us in heavily weighted, unspoken fear.

Indeed she might have left him, but what is worse; an unfulfilled miserable woman who is wondering about her own ability to have children, a woman who feels betrayed because the man she loves didn't tell her the truth, or a woman who is on the same page and is relieved not to be confronted with her own desire not to have children?

Of course, what this young man failed to realize is that unfulfilled desires come back to haunt couples. She would leave him if she discovered he had lied to her by omission. She would be miserable if she couldn't have children and blame him for her loss. Conversations like these have to happen in order for a relationship to be healthy and sound. So men and women might as well jump into the difficult conversation arena right from the beginning.

The discussion about what women do and do not want to do sexually is a case in point. Men are not mind readers. It is better to assume that they want to go further than their partners, is generally a matter of fact that both men and women should acknowledge. It is way better to be up front and uncomfortable than to be raped. It is much safer to assume that men will push forward as a general rule than to set yourself up in a difficult situation because you assumed he would be a gentleman. He might be a gentleman, he also might not be. If you rest your safety on an assumption, you might get in real trouble. Why risk finding out the hard way that he doesn't think self-control is an asset.

In all aspects of life, men and women have to be personally responsible for the way they set up their lives. If, in the past, you have put yourself into a position in which you were raped, that does not mean that you were at fault – victims of rape are *never* at fault. That means you didn't know how to protect yourself and made the mistake of believing that everyone shared your values and could be trusted. We'll discuss this later. What it does mean is that you must make no assumptions, you must take care to protect yourself in the future. Many women who have been date raped once, have been date raped more than once. Are they dumb? No. They are loving and hopeful.

Both men and women have similar unspoken fears of rejection that play out around talking frankly with each other concerning the most important aspects of their relationships. It isn't always easy, because everyone faces the risk of disagreement. No matter how wonderful a relationship is, there will always be disagreement – it's a fact of life. So if you disagree about how far you are willing to go, that's just a warm-up for the rest of the disagreements that will follow. How you handle disagreement is the measure of your maturity.

Popular media plays straight into those rejection fears. "Ten things you shouldn't tell your boyfriend…" recently appeared as a headline on Yahoo. What's that all about? Frank talk with the people you are dating is vital to protecting yourself against things you do and don't want to do. Frank conversation is also vital to protecting both of you from getting into trouble if you run into an irreconcilable difference. Unless you talk frankly with each other, both of you are going to make assumptions, and those assumptions could be exceedingly harmful.

Whether you're talking about having children, agreeing on future goals or agreeing to have sex together - now or later - the important things in life need to be talked about and agreed upon at each step. They must be discussed *before the fact*. If they are discussed, you can maintain healthy relationships. If they are not discussed, unspoken assumptions become the traps for later relationship failure, sexual aggression or rape.

Having said that, let me point out that there are men all over this world who believe they are entitled to have intercourse with the woman of their choice, regardless of what that woman wants. Conversations with these men are useless. You must protect yourself from them by sticking with other people whenever you are with them. If you don't want to take a chance of being raped, never allow yourself to be alone with a man in a situation where you are vulnerable. Do not put yourself at risk simply because you are a nice person and everyone *should* respect you, or because you're young, or because you're a virgin. Figure out how to protect yourself in advance. Make certain that you double date. Make certain that you surround yourself with family or friends. Don't go into dangerous places (jogging in Central Park in New York City after dark, for example) unless you go in a pack – and stay in the pack. Don't allow yourself to be alone with any male (friend, family member, family friend or date) if you don't know them well enough to trust them. Even if you think you can trust them, think twice. Never assume you can trust anyone. These statements are not about all men being bad. These statements are about being proactively protective of yourself and of him – being personally responsible for your own safety. That is a very mature and responsible thing to do. The male reasoning is often, "If she didn't want it, why did she go to my room?" The percentage of sex abuse and rape is high enough, particularly for women between the ages of 16 and 26 to warrant being cautions at all times.

Do you think that's crazy thinking? Recently an eleven year old CHILD was gang raped by eight men - the oldest man was 26 - and the community condemned the CHILD as, "asking for it" because she dressed like a sexy twenty-one year old. Children do not ask to be gang raped. No one asks to be gang raped. If that child went to school buck naked she was not asking to be gang raped. But that was the thinking of the guilty parties as reported by the New York Times – which also held that eleven year old child responsible for being raped by adults.

Now, chances are that you're not going to be vigilant against rape at all times, and there certainly are men who it's safe to be alone with. The point of this book is to make you very aware of what could possibly happen to you while dating and to give you tools for dealing with the repercussions of date rape. It is certainly not written to make you a neurotic mess who doesn't trust any man and who never leaves her apartment. However, one in eight college women are raped, and one in four are sexually abused, so date rape is a problem you have to be aware of and protect against.

The most important piece of advice in this book is to be proactive in keeping yourself safe. Listen to your intuition. If you have the slightest doubt about being alone with someone – even someone you've known for a long time – pay attention. You have subtle skills for reading body language that comes from centuries of women being the victims of rape and abuse. Read The Rape of the Sabin Women[1] to see how rape is celebrated in our earliest literature – hint the women liked it and chose to stay with their rapists. Of course the rapists wrote the history.

Women have always been preyed upon and instinctively know how to look for signs of danger. If your intuition warns you that something is "not right," don't override or ignore it. Even if it seems silly, don't take a chance. Even if you have a million dates in your life, there's no rule that says you have to accommodate *any* of them sexually and risk danger to yourself.

A word to men who think women want to be raped. Rape is a felony. If the woman decides to prosecute, that's the end of all your plans and dreams for the future. If your parents have invested huge amounts of their hard earned cash in your education, you can kiss their investment goodbye. If, by some strange twist of thought you decide to use date rape drugs – you fail to ask your date if she's on

---

[1] The Rape of the Sabin Women:
http://en.wikipedia.org/wiki/The_Rape_of_the_Sabine_Women

prescription medicine, and the drugs have a negative interaction, or if the drug mixes negatively with the amount of alcohol she has ingested – you can face the possibility of murder charges. Is an orgasm worth the risk? Is the fulfillment of a sexual fantasy worth the damage it can do to your life? Is it worth the damage you do to the woman? If you love the woman, is it worth the damage it does to your relationship? Think about it. Date rape is the quickest way I know to end a relationship. Is that what you want to do?

If you are a woman who is thinking of a career in the armed services[2] or overseas with a company like Kellogg Brown and Root[3] – think long and hard about being raped or abused particular in a military notorious for not protecting its women. As of this writing, these organizations, and I suspect many other large corporations, do not protect their female employees from sexual harassment and rape. And, they have made them sign arbitration agreements so they do not have legal redress for what was done to them after the fact and cannot not prosecute the perpetrators of the rape. Joining the armed services or working for these large companies is kind of like going out with mass murderer Ted Bundy[4] and expecting nothing bad to happen.

This book talks about how to avoid date or acquaintance rape, the profile of the average acquaintance rapist, what to do after you have been raped and how to

---

[2] Armed Services Article:
http://www.msnbc.msn.com/id/41598622/ns/us_news-life/
[3] Kellogg Brown and Root:
http://abcnews.go.com/Blotter/story?id=4099514&page=1
[4] Ted Bundy: http://en.wikipedia.org/wiki/Ted_Bundy

recover from the experience. Date rape is a huge problem. Women in America are raped every two minutes. 80% of all rapes are committed by someone the victim knows.

Chapter 1
How I Got Date Raped

Date rape is very personal for me. Years ago, when I was still in college, I went out for a cup of coffee with a lifeguard I had met at the beach where I swam every day while visiting my grandparents during spring break. In those days I was very self-confident, utterly naive and a little rebellious. I loved being with my grandparents, but I also thought a little social life would be nice.

On the way home my date pulled onto a golf course near my home and kissed me. It was nice and I didn't think much about it – parking was the norm in those days and until that day I had never experienced repercussions. In the past, my dates and I would neck, we'd fool around, but we always stopped when I had reached my sexual boundaries. My sexual boundaries had shrunk over the years, but no matter how far we went, my dates had always remained within my comfort zone. I expected the man I was with to stop when I said, "No." This man didn't stop. I definitely said, "No." I struggled, I fought hard, but he was very strong and pinned me under the steering wheel so I couldn't escape and then he raped me.

When I thought back to the event – rape victims always replay the event to see what they should have done differently – I remembered something very interesting. That man had asked me out in the presence of two other lifeguards. I had caught a look between those two men that didn't "look right." *And I didn't pay attention.* At the time, I wondered what that look was about, but I didn't listen to my intuition. One of the things I teach now is, if something doesn't "look right" – pay attention – it probably isn't right. Do not override your intuition. It's better to say no to the date and be disappointed that a dating opportunity didn't work out, than to be unable to say no to the rape. If someone picks you up in his car, you are in his territory and in his territory you are at risk. I'll talk more about that later.

I have great protective abilities when it comes to dealing with unpleasant experiences. I decided not to be traumatized. I deliberately put what happened behind me. I compartmentalized it. I buried it deep. Although I tell my sister almost everything, I didn't tell her about being raped for more than 40 years. I rarely thought about it and didn't talk about it. It was just something that happened, and in some ways it was less traumatic than other things that I found more threatening and more unpleasant in subsequent years.

Later, I came to understand that we all deal with our traumas in different ways. I discovered that in a class where we had to talk about "the worst thing we had ever done." Several women talked about being date or acquaintance raped. These were not young women, and the rapes were not recent, but they had branded these women for life. Statistically, many women are traumatized for 15 or 20 years after a rape. The women in this class lived and relived the experience. The betrayal still brought tears to their eyes and lumps to their throats. For them it was an ongoing event. In that class the teachers kept saying, "You are innocent." "It was not your fault." But the tears still flowed, and when the women talked about the event, their bodies cringed. Notice that they question was about the worst thing *you* have ever done – not the worst thing that was ever done to you.

Still more years later, when I learned how to create guided meditations, and understood that carefully structured processes could rid rape victims of the continuous violation they had experienced, I set about to spread the word. I structured my work in three directions – preventing rapes by being proactively careful, getting over the violation in the case of rape and protecting against additional violation in the future.

As I've already said, women who have been violated once are often violated again. There are a number of reasons for this. They are attracted to the rapist personality. The dominating male is very attractive and, without guidance, women who are attracted to this kind of man never develop the skills to avoid rape and protect themselves. Women who are raped more than once want to believe that the people they love, and who love them, won't do that to them. They want to believe in their personal safety and their inherent right to trust the men they love, and are sometimes very naïve about the situations they get themselves into. Again, you don't have to stay home forever, but you also can't go into "his territory" alone or invite him into your territory alone. Just make that a rule.

From almost the moment I developed a woman's body, and for most of my life, I felt as if I was engaged in a surrealistic sexual obstacle course. Men would rub up against me in subways, or pat my ass as I walked down the street. Friends of the family, and my mother's boyfriends in particular, would proposition me or stick their tongues in my ear. On many dates, in meetings, even in filing rooms at offices, I would find myself fending off unwanted sexual approaches. Married men, boyfriends of friends, old men, young men – you name it – would pat, paw, kiss and whatever without invitation. Marriage didn't protect me from unwanted attention, getting fat didn't protect me and getting old didn't protect me.

I finally figured out that if I didn't want to lock myself in my room forever, I should figure out what to do about the problem of unwanted sexual attention. I learned how to regularly create mental and emotional boundaries. I now assume that I need to take precautions without resenting them. I learned about the Second Chakra, which governs your sex organs and sexuality. When I don't want to be approached by anyone I say, "I now close my Second Chakra." If I want to be approached, I say, "I now open my Second Chakra." You'd be amazed at how well those openings and closings work.

The difficulty with the Chakras is the middle ground, when you don't want to be invisible to the opposite sex; you just want to avoid sexual abuse or rape. My second strategy was to become very outspoken. There is never any doubt about what I want and don't want. I am very clear about my comfort zone – and yes, I still have a comfort zone as an older woman. If someone I don't invite into my personal space approaches me and doesn't respond to direct communication, I get obnoxiously loud and very demeaning in my rejection.

Chapter 2

Reality Check
This Can Happen To You

One night, when I was in boarding school in the 1950s, the girls in our dorm got together after hours and started talking. I would consider us a group of very protected young women. We were in a prestigious boarding school. We all came from money and privilege. We came from good neighborhoods and, if I were to take an educated guess, had never been in a bad neighborhood in our lives even for a walk. Yet, not one person in that group had escaped some form of sexual aggression from a male that they knew well – not one. None of us admitted to being raped, but all of us had been traumatized by the men around us.

Here are some statistics:

*   Two thirds of American women have been the victims of unwanted sexual aggression or rape.

*   Women 16 to 19 are the most victimized group when it comes to sexual aggression.

*   Women 20 to 24 come in a close second. These two age groups are four times more at risk of being raped or abused than any other age group.

*   Women aren't the only victims of rape. 10% of rapes occur in males of that same age group, 16-24.

*   80% of women in high school have been victimized by some kind of sexual aggression during high school dating. These experiences run the gamut from being forced to physically do something sexual they didn't want to do, to attempted rape or actual rape.

*   One in four college women have been the victims of attempted rape and one in eight have actually been raped.

*   One in four college men have forcefully attempted to engage in sexual intercourse against someone's will. In spite of crying, pleading, begging and fighting – more than half have succeeded in raping their victims.

*   80% of the women raped were assaulted by a close acquaintance or date – on average, someone they have known for close to a year.

*   Nearly half of the men who raped these women were first dates, casual dates or people with whom the victims had been romantically involved over time. Others included roommate's boyfriends, boyfriend's friends, mother's dates or mother's boyfriends, classmates, friends of the family, co-workers, religious leaders and even relatives like fathers, brothers and uncles.

*   In the case of college rapes, most of the violations occurred off campus.

*   Half the rapes occurred on what can be called, "the man's turf" – his apartment, his car or his house.

*   Over 50% of the rapes occurred during or at the end of a planned date.

People at greatest risk of rape are those who are in denial. "It can't happen to me," is the most dangerous thing anyone can think. If they hide behind the assumption that they are too old, too fat, too unattractive, they are in trouble. No one wants to think of themselves as a potential rape victim. Why would anyone want to rape them? Their behavior is exemplary. They're nice people. They know these men. They are nice men with similar values. The men you have dated have always stopped before – even the man you are with has always stopped before. That kind of thinking results in one in eight women between the ages of 16 and 24 being raped. Women in their 80s have been raped. Women in all shapes and sizes have been raped. Simply put, the statistics don't support that kind of denial. The very thing that women think protects them may be the thing that attracts the rapist. Make no assumptions when it comes to your vulnerability to sexual abuse.

No man, no matter how well you think you know him, no matter how well he thinks he knows himself, comes with a guarantee that he won't do something to you that you don't want him to do.

You are in greatest danger of sexual assault and date rape when you have convinced yourself that it can't happen to you. Because that is the moment you let your guard down and take risks. In order to prevent date rape, you must understand it and do your best to prevent it before you become a statistic. Even if it doesn't seem right or fair, you must always be on your guard and must not put yourself into a situation where you are vulnerable.

If you have already experienced date rape or unwanted sexual aggression by a man you dated, you loved, you trusted, or you simply have known, you must be aware that there is another side to the seemingly trustworthy men around you. Does this seem unfair to the men you know and love? Well, there are nice men – 7 in 8 won't rape you, 3 in 4 won't get aggressive with you … but 80% of college women can attest to the 1 in 4 who will.

Most of us who were victims of such things find ourselves living with guilt, shame, anger, outrage, fear, lack of trust and even despair. I've written this book and created numerous visualization and meditation processes to help victims literally put the guilt, shame and rage behind them and emerge from the experience safe, alert, healed, and able to let go of those paralyzing victim feelings. Many women who have experienced rape don't trust themselves. Guided visualizations can renew your trust in yourself. Not blind trust, but *informed* trust.

Does this mean forgiving the rapist? It does not. What these processes do mean is making certain that the rapist isn't repeating his crime endlessly in your head. It means taking action in your own behalf. It means putting the traumatic memories away where you don't constantly relive them. Rape is an unforgivable act, made more unforgivable by the reliving of the crime long after it is over. Reliving that crime is like being raped over and over again.

Finally, remember that experience I had in high school when all of us came forward with our tales of sexual abuse? That conversation taught me that I was not alone in my experiences. If 80% of all college women have been, or will be, the victims of sexual assault, hadn't you better talk about the risk with your friends? Build support groups within your school community, talk to each other about what is dangerous and what to avoid. Help each other to remain safe by sticking together and, if one of you falls victim to a sexual predator – a rapist is a sexual predator, even when you know and like him – help your friend go to the police, or the hospital. Help her go through the process of dealing with what has happened to her. Help her deal with the possibility of pregnancy or disease. Help her take action to bring the rapist to justice. That's what friends are for. You never know when you, yourself, will need such a friend.

If you know someone who has been raped or abused, don't avoid them, embrace them. Your friend needs you now more than ever before. They need your support. When I was in college, one of the girls on campus "slept" with all 29 members of a fraternity in one night. No one that I knew bothered to ask if she did it willingly – everyone leapt to judgment that she was a "bad person."

Can you imagine happily and willingly giving your body to 29 men standing in a line waiting to violate you? Can you imagine what they must have been saying – because the activity wouldn't have been quiet – there would have been peer pressure, and cheering each other on. It would have been very degrading for the woman. It would have been a gang rape. At the time, I stood in judgment with the rest of the school. I didn't offer her understanding or friendship. And I regret that because I now understand that women don't always do things like that willingly. Even if something like that starts willingly, it often doesn't end that way.

My father's death and my being raped happened in close proximity to each other and are strangely linked in my mind. I handled both events by burying them deeply behind strongly locked emotional doors. I remember when my father died – in my senior year at college – everyone seemed to avoid me. They didn't know what to say, so they said nothing. Finally, one woman I hardly knew stopped me in the hall and said, "I don't know what to say to you, but if you want to talk, I'd be glad to listen." That was 52 years ago, and I can still see her face. I don't think we had ever spoken before that moment, and we didn't become friends, but I still vividly remember feeling the kindness in her words. A little kindness goes a very long way.

Sometimes victims of rape or abuse need to talk, sometimes they need quiet time with someone who just shares space with them – but they need to know they are not wrong, they are not guilty, they are not to blame, and they are still loved and appreciated by their friends. They need to know they're okay, and that they can feel okay about themselves. As often as not, acceptance from the outside leads to healing and acceptance from the inside. The victims of sexual aggression and rape are not guilty. It's not their fault that they were raped. And you can help them.

One more thing. Actual penetration does not have to occur for harm to be done. Another friend of mine was grabbed by a stranger, forced into a mailroom in her building and, although she was not actually raped, was so terrified that she was scarred for life.

Putting rape or sexual aggression behind you is very possible. It's a decision – a choice. You may have been raped or abused, but you don't have to continue being raped or abused in your mind. You can shut the door and never open it again. No one has to keep revisiting crimes against themselves in their memories.

What is Date Rape?

Simply put, date rape is any unwanted sexual encounter in which penetration occurs. Sexual aggression can be equally traumatic, even when penetration is not part of the scenario. It's very important, if we are to protect ourselves and our friends against date rape that we understand what rape is, and what it isn't. For the purposes of this book, I shall be talking about rape victims as women. However, men can and do get raped as well. For the most part men who are raped get raped by men. However, when the victim is too young to legally choose to have intercourse, women can be guilty of rape as well.

Rape is not limited to the penis. Any object inserted into the vagina or anus – or in some cases the mouth – can constitute rape. Men and women can be equally guilty of sexual abuse.

Also separate from this discussion is sexual harassment – when a man or woman is forced to grant sexual favors in return for promotions or to simply to keep their jobs (I say men can be victims, but again, men are usually the perpetrators of that kind of abuse and women are generally the victims).

Finally there is marital rape, where sex is forced on an unwilling partner usually at least once every day. It is actually normal to think that what is being done to you by your husband must be all right because you're married and because usually your husband follows the abuse with making up and saying how much he loves you. You have the right to say no even within the context of marriage.

Forced, Unwanted Sex is Date Rape

When a man has sexual intercourse (with his penis or another object) with a woman or another man after she or he has communicated with words or actions that the intercourse is unwanted, that man has committed rape. It makes no difference whether that man is a stranger, an acquaintance, a friend, a lover or even a husband. It makes no difference if she has permitted him to "park" with her. It makes no difference if she has had consensual sex with him or someone else in the past. It makes no difference if she is sober, alert and aware or drunk, stoned, asleep or unconscious. If the man's penis (or an object wielded by him) penetrates her vagina, or his or her anus, or mouth when he or she is unwilling – unable – or too young to give consent – that's rape. If that man tries to penetrate against his or her will, but is stopped in the act, that's attempted rape.

There are two kinds of rape – stranger rape and acquaintance rape.

* Stranger rape is a crime in which the victim doesn't know the rapist. Stranger rape is often accompanied by violence and sometimes murder. This kind of rape makes the nightly news and is the crime that women take self-defense courses to prevent. To avert this kind of rape, women install multiple door locks, put bars on their windows, buy pistols for their nightstands and carry Mace in their purses. Yet, stranger rape accounts for only 20% of all rapes.

* Acquaintance rape – date rape – accounts for 80% of all rapes. Someone the victim knows rapes her. 50% of those rapes occur on a date. Rapists might be a classmate, co-worker, teacher, employer, superior

officer or relative. He may be your roommate's brother, someone you met at a party, your boyfriend's best friend or even your mother's boyfriend or husband. I know many women who were raped by their fathers, uncles and brothers. The date rapist may be someone you are dating – casually or steadily – someone with whom you have been romantically involved or even physically intimate in the past. The list includes your husband, your lover, or live-in partner.

How can your husband rape his wife? Simple - Rape occurs after the victim has said, "No."

Our Culture Encourages Rape

Our culture does nothing to stop rape, it actually encourages it. Think about all those romance novels in which the heroine is raped, falls in love with and marries her rapist. If rape and dominance started the relationship, chances are it will continue into the relationship.

All rape is devastating. Stranger rape is usually terrifying, while date rape is more often a heartbreaking betrayal – although it can also develop into terrifying brutality. Both forms of rape are horrendous acts for the victim.

Non-consensual sex or sexual assault is never innocent on the part of the perpetrator – no matter how he may justify it to himself and his friends. There was a time when the victims were always blamed for what happened to them. All the perp's friends would show up in court and swear that she had slept with them as well. They would come up with all the temptations she had offered him. If she hadn't worn a short skirt... If she hadn't gotten into his car... If she hadn't been "asking for it"... If she hadn't flirted... If she hadn't gone to his room... You name it... none of that would have happened to her. Just like eleven year old child, just like spousal abuse, there is always a "reason" to justify the rape. And in the mind of the abuser, it's always the victim's fault. In those days, the victim was at fault in the eyes of the court and particularly in the eyes of the police. Things have changed in many ways since those days. At least it has changed in some places. In the military and on many college campuses it doesn't seem to have caught on yet.

Date Rape is a Crime

Like most victims of date rape, I didn't go to the police and report the crime. I didn't go to a rape crisis center, a physician or a counselor. Like most women who have been raped by men they know even casually, I failed to see myself as the victim of a crime. I saw myself as guilty of not preventing something I didn't want and didn't ask for.

Rape is the most underreported crime in America (if not the world). According to government agency estimates, three to ten rapes or attempted rapes actually occur for every rape that is reported to the police – I personally believe it is closer to 10 than to three. One study found that in group of fifteen hundred college women who were victims of rape or attempted rape only 5% ever reported the crime to law enforcement or college authorities. Experts believe that possibly only 10% of all rapes are reported to the police.

Today I believe that what I failed to do – failing to report the rape to the police – was wrong. I left in place a man who was a rapist and who, by his position as a life guard had access to many women and would be trusted by most of them because he saved lives. I'm quite certain I wasn't his only victim, and by leaving him in place I put other women at risk. It took years for me to understand that what was done to me was a crime. In fairness, this rape occurred in the '60s, when even the police didn't think date rape without injury or death was much of a crime. In most communities, the victim was believed to be guilty even by the authorities. In a recent study 62% of date rape victims didn't understand that what was done to them was a crime.

However, what I failed to do back in the '60s left a predator out in the public arena so that he could rape and rape again – which I'm quite sure he did. Without the deterrent of consequences, there is no reason for people who have rapist tendencies not to rape. As recently as 2011, conservative representatives in the House of Representatives in Washington, DC tried to decriminalize rape unless the woman is violently abused. So far they have not succeeded. It is up to us to prevent them. Fortunately voters have kept the worst of the offenders out of office and I certainly hope it stays that way.

In the courts today, the law takes a different view of rape – except when it comes to minorities in certain states. Unwanted sexual intercourse – even when committed by a date, acquaintance, relative or husband – is legally a felony.

Using an object to penetrate a victim – so the rapist can claim that he didn't "have sex" with the victim – is also a felony. Having sex with someone with diminished capacity (unconscious, seriously drunk, drugged, low IQ or underage) is also a felony.

Why is rape held by so many people to be unpleasant, but okay? Just look at our media. Four major rape crimes that were covered by the mass media in the past decade give us pause. The first was the William Kennedy Smith case – in which he had non-consensual sex with a woman he met in a bar. He had good lawyers and got off without going to jail. The next is more problematic. The second widely published case was the Duke Lacrosse team, several members of which were found innocent (after years in court) of raping an exotic dancer. According to DNA testing, the victim was found to have slept with other men in that time frame, with no DNA evidence of any members of the Lacrosse team having violated her. Evidently the district attorney in that case had known about the DNA for some time, and still prosecuted those students. The district attorney lost his license in that little bit of headline-grabbing, judicial excess. Most recently, as I mentioned earlier, an 11 year old girl was gang raped by eight men and was blamed for provoking the rape with her clothing choices. Finally there was the case of Jamie Leigh Jones[5] who was drugged and gang raped by a group of KBR contractors only four days after she went to work for Kellogg Brown and Root in Iraq. Unfortunately she had

---

[5] Jamie Leigh Jones"http://www.motherjones.com/politics/2011/07/kbr-could-win-jamie-leigh-jones-rape-trial

signed an arbitration agreement as part of her contract and had lost her ability to sue. None of these famous cases were well resolved, or fair. Two of the cases were tried in Texas which does not promise to turn out well for a woman or a child who is a minority.

The popular media is irresponsible in the extreme. Newspapers have been known to make the victim guilty. Pop culture media like soap operas, or romance novels – portray date and even spousal rape as passionate guys getting carried away and women who start out resistant and end up loving their abuser – sort of like the way most average date rapists think of themselves and their victims. In most instances of fictional story telling, the female victim ends up living happily ever after with her rapist. That's not art imitating life. That's art imitating wishful thinking. I know several women who married their rapists and the rape continued for years, with the violation becoming more and more violent. That's what homes for battered women are all about.

In another arena, in my years with the National Emergency Care Advisory Council, I monitored popular television shows and reported emergency care errors to the Program Practices Departments of NBC, ABC and CBS. Included in the shows I monitored was the much-touted "Emergency." In all those years, I never once saw a correct first aid procedure, even on "Emergency." And, I saw the results of such incorrect procedure in the field. Television and movies claim to represent the "reality of what's happening in the world." They do not claim that they actually research what correct procedure is and they do not regard themselves as instructional. That's why they represent the point of view of the rapist and popular culture, which says, "She *was* asking for it." Or even worse, "She *must have been* asking for it." Shows follow the insane belief that, "Everything will be okay if he just marries her in the end," which means that for the rest of the marriage, she's going to have to deal with a man who thinks raping her is acceptable. It's a formula for disaster for the woman. It's also a closed loop. Media imitates the people who imitate the media, who imitate the people imitating the media. And it is not harmless.

Date Rape Is Also a Power Issue

I don't believe for a minute that date rape isn't about sex – it is. It is also about power. If men drive cars and tote guns to show off their masculinity – of course they rape for the same reason. Many men who force women to have sex with them have subscribed to the Neanderthal image of males. These come in three basic attitudes.

1. **"I am the king and what I say goes" attitude**. These men are strongly identified with the myth of male dominance and female subservience. Any man who is so identified is a potential rapist. However he learned this role, he accepts as truth the idea that a woman will only respect a man who will "lay down the law" to her. He believes that he has to show her who's boss or she will henpeck him. His rape is not because he's just carried away by his passion – he rapes because he needs to assert his power. He needs to overcome, to conquer, women.

He sees women as potential adversaries for his superiority. If this kind of man completely buys into using force, hostility and violence to express his need for power, chances are he will humiliate and hurt his victims.

2. **"I am a man of action" attitude.** Men who act first and think later are generally not very personally responsible in most aspects of their lives. They charge recklessly into all types of situations – rape being only one – without ever considering the consequences of their acts. They pursue their whims and urges without exercising self-control or self-discipline. These men are a hazard to themselves, as well as their dates. They pursue their desires without considering the obvious legal and emotional consequences they may face in the years and months to come.

3. **"I want what I want when I want it!" attitude**. This kind of rapist usually is pathological – he lacks a social conscience. He acts for himself with little regard for others. "Get out of my way or you'll get hurt," is his core belief. If you get hurt, that's "your tough luck." In a sexual situation, this man is oblivious to the consequences of any physical or emotional pain he causes his victim. He just goes for what he wants.

These attitudes aren't worn like signs or T-shirts. If they were, no self-respecting woman would ever go near a potential rapist. But these are the tendencies that lurk beneath the surface of a surprising number of men that most of us would consider "normal." And if you take into consideration the addition of peer pressure, and the loss of judgment brought on by alcohol that accompanies many situations leading to rape, you see part of the scope of the problem. Rape is a sexual fantasy. The majority of men have admitted in surveys that they would rape if they could be assured of not being caught and punished.

Chapter 3
Myths About Women and Sex

The myths, perpetuated by society and aided by the media, support potential rapists in their justification for sexually abusing their dates, girlfriends and wives. These myths are used by men to legitimize their behavior before, during and after the event. These are myths – they have nothing to do with reality and they are not an excuse under the law.

Myth 1.
Women really want to be raped. This is a sexual fantasy that men who are sexually aggressive yearn to make a reality to let them off the hook. In fact, women actually yearn to be loved, cared for and treasured. They do not want to be raped. "Entertainment" media often presents women as sex objects who are supposed to play out these rape fantasies. The media presents women as objects to be

raped – as objects whose sole reason for being is to provide men's sexual stimulus. Men who buy this myth convince themselves that women enjoy being dominated – sexually and in every other way. They believe that women get turned on when men play rough. They believe that when a woman says "no," she doesn't mean it. Even worse, they convince themselves that if the woman really didn't want it, she could stop him because, "no woman can ever be raped against her will." They believe that subconsciously, all women enjoy being conquered. That level of ignorance goes right along with Republican Candidate Todd Aiken's "legitimate rape" quote in which he stated that women who are raped can't get pregnant because the body prevents pregnancy if it's legitimate rape. There is a colossal amount of ignorance in this world. Money and power do nothing to make people smart.

That is a myth. *No woman wants to be sexually assaulted. EVER. And women are the weaker sex…in many cases, they can't stop an aggressive male and they do want to. And there is no such thing as women preventing pregnancy simply because they are being raped.*

Myth 2.
Men can't control themselves sexually the way women can. In order to justify their behavior, men have circulated the myth that men can only "make out" for a certain amount of time before they "cross the line" and lose control. After they have crossed that line, they are "not responsible for their actions." In other words, it's not his fault that he raped his date. It's her fault for not knowing

that he could only go for so long without losing control. To the degree that it's difficult for women to believe that a man can't control himself or wouldn't warn her that he was at a breaking point where he is in danger of losing control, there is a level of reality to that lie – the reality is that after a certain point men stop being willing to control themselves – not that they can't control themselves, they simply don't…Which is why women really have to be defensive.

That is a myth. *Men have as much control over their sexuality as they have over their eating habits. Sexuality should not be confused with pooping – in which most men can control themselves long enough to find a toilet. There are many ways to relieve sexual tension that do not include rape.*

Myth 3.

Women are required to have sex with men who spend money on them. This is a common belief, even among junior high school-age males. 51% of junior high school boys and 41% of junior high school girls believe that a man has a right to force a woman to kiss him if he has spent "a lot" of money on her. 25% of the boys and 17% of the girls say sex is okay if the man has spent a lot of money on the girl. That's the old prostitute legend in which women are expected to "put out" in return for payment in real money or gifts – like dinner and a movie.

That is a myth. *The vast majority of women are not whores. They do not go out on dates with the understanding that they will be expected to perform sexually before the* *evening is over if the male pays enough for the favor. Men who subscribe to this belief should make their demands clear to their date at the outset. Women who do not wish to perform sexually should be given a choice. Women should also make it clear that they are not for sale. That is definitely not a respectful behavior on the man's part and should NEVER be accepted by a woman.*

Myth 4.

Women say "no," but their actions say "yes."
Many men claim to be mind readers. They claim that women wear sexy clothes because they want sex. They claim that women flirt because they want sex. They claim that women cuddle because they want sex. They claim that women accept an invitation to the man's apartment because they want sex. They claim that women play hard to get in order to turn the man on because in their heart of hearts women really want sex. They claim that by raping a woman, they "only gave her what she *really* wanted."

That is a myth. *Men can't read women's minds, they can only interpret what they think a woman is thinking and they often do that in accordance with what they want the woman to be thinking.*

In truth, women generally dress to please their own eye, and in accordance with their culture and the trends of the day. Women may flirt, but that is no more an invitation to sex than yawning. A simple kiss goodnight – or even a very passionate kiss goodnight – is not an open invitation to rape. Kissing and petting are not preludes to the "main

event" unless the woman wants them to be. No one "asks for it" unless they ask for it in just that many words…
Here's the kicker: women have the right to change their minds even at the last second. Women can change their minds even if they are in bed and naked and "totally ready to go…"

Myth 5.

Because the woman is not a virgin, it's not rape.
Going back to junior high, 33% of junior high school students surveyed saw nothing wrong with raping a woman who was already sexually active. This reflects an attitude in the popular culture that once a woman has lost her virginity, there is "no harm done" if she is forced to have sex because she's already "bad".

That is a myth. *No matter how many sexual experiences a woman has had, forced sex is rape. The other side of "no," is a felony.*

Chapter 4

Date Rape is Not Pleasurable
Even if You Love the Rapist

Date Rape is Violent

A man who will rape a woman has the potential of getting physically violent and even killing his victim. There's nothing safe about rape or physical aggression. There's nothing innocent about rape or sexual aggression. Many women and girls are murdered every year attempting to resist sexual aggression as well as both physical and mental domination.

Here are the statistics:

* 87% of rapists either carry weapons or threaten violence or death to their victims. In a study of college women who had experienced sexual

aggression, various levels of violence were experienced.

* 48% of the victims reported that the perpetrators simply ignored their protests and requests to stop.

* 32% of the offenders verbally coerced their victims into offensive or displeasing behavior.

* 15% used physical restraint.

* 6% used threats or physical aggression.

Date Rape is Hurtful, Immoral and Criminal

Date rape can physically scar a person for life, but it is more likely to emotionally scar them. It is a betrayal of a woman's trust – or a man's trust if the victim is a man. It leaves the victim distrusting men. It leaves them distrusting themselves and their own judgment.

In recent years, the victims of sexual predators in the Catholic Church have made headlines. 30, 40, 50 years after they were abused, men and women are still feeling victimized by their priest-abusers. "Oh, but that's because they trusted their priest," you point out. Yes, that's because they trusted their priest – and their date, their boyfriend, and their friend's brother, their father, uncle, their mother's boyfriend, and anyone else who acquaintance raped or violated them. Rape is a cruel crime. That's why it's a felony.

One more thing: If the rape is incest, generally the mother has an idea that something is going on no matter how much she may protest that she doesn't, and she doesn't stop it. So incest is a double betrayal....or quadruple if you consider the betrayal of the mother as well.

Just notice how rape has been headlined in the U.S. Armed Services recently. Female soldiers in Iraq cannot go to the bathroom alone at night for fear of being raped – If I know about it don't you think the armed services officers in charge of protecting those women should know about it? Where recruiters and senior officers have preyed on girls in their sphere of influence nothing was done about it.

Notice how women in the contracting companies like Halliburton/KBR are raped by their fellow employees and nothing is done about it. In fact in at least one case the evidence kit from the rape was "lost." Notice how soldiers in Nigeria and Congo, India and many countries in South and Central America – to name a few – use rape as a war tactic. The ultimate "holding the woman responsible" happens in the Arab nations, like Saudi Arabia, where recently a woman who was gang raped was ordered to receive 200 lashes for *her* "crime." Rape is a very strange crime and women have to be very proactive to avoid it.

Chapter 5

How To Avoid Date Rape

The victims of date rape usually ask two questions, "What did I do wrong?" and "How could I have prevented what happened?" These are questions to ask *before* a rape. These are also questions to ask before you go out again after you've been raped. The best time to take steps to prevent date rape is before it happens.

There is life after date rape. Most women and men who have been victims of this crime do not lock themselves in their homes forever. Most often they move on in their lives; most often, but not always. It is important to move on. It is also important to understand that there are precautions you can take to spare yourself the pain and consequences of rape.

Guidelines For Women

1. Set Your Boundaries and Communicate Them.

You want to get clear with yourself and everyone you date how far you want to go. Think about it beforehand and communicate it in advance. You don't want to be making decisions about boundaries and limits under pressure in the back seat of a car. You don't want your date to be confronted with those limits for the first time under similar pressure. If you don't set those boundaries before you get into a situation that's difficult to control, the sexually aggressive man may make the decision for you.

This isn't about introducing yourself, "Hi, my name is Joan, and I don't want to go all the way with you." That would make no sense. But when the choice about getting into the car alone, or going to his apartment alone has to be made, that's when you say, "I'm not comfortable doing that. I'm concerned that you may misunderstand it and think that I might be interested in sex. I'm not and I need to set that parameter before I go – Or I should not go." Does that sound like an excuse for the man to say to himself, "If she's mentioning sex that must mean she wants it?" Well, men do think like that, and if you are worried that the conversation will be misunderstood – don't ride in the car and don't go to his room. Find a nearby café and insist that you meet there. If you have even a slight thought that he might misunderstand that could be your intuition at work. Remember, you do have an intuition and if your intuition is screaming even in a small voice in your head – listen.

I would suggest you listen to my Creative Visualization process "Creating Boundaries." This process suggests steps to your subconscious to set firm mental boundaries and makes communicating those boundaries easier. It makes life simpler for both you and your date if you can be very clear in your communication. It also builds self-esteem so that you feel more confident when setting those boundaries. Simply moving a man's hand away from the places you don't want him to touch may not be strong enough for an aggressive man. "No. Touching me there is not all right with me," is a great deal clearer. "Don't do that," is also clear. "I really like that," is another clear message. Communicating what you do like and will accept is a great way of reinforcing statements about what you don't like and won't accept. Remember everything on the other side of "No," is illegal.

2. Avoid Men Who Have Bought into the Male Myths.

In the following pages, I outlined the kind of man who is most apt to push your sexual boundaries. Don't feel obliged to date this kind of man. When they ask you out, refuse or at least insist that the date be a double or pack date. There are a number of indicators that you should watch out for:

A. He abuses you emotionally by insulting you or belittling you alone and with other people. He may call it teasing, but if it's uncomfortable and negative, it's abuse. He doesn't listen to you, ignores your opinions, or gets upset if you take the lead in the relationship. Watch out for phrases like, "just kidding," or "I'm just being sarcastic," after a particularly hurtful barb. Men who play games that aren't really funny are men who mask what they do as innocent. These are men who will blame you for miscommunication, or will try to convince you that you were actually "asking" to be raped.

B. He refuses to allow you to share in the decisions or expenses of a date. He gets angry if you suggest an activity or offer to pay. He insists on being in charge of the relationship. He insists on dominating you right from the beginning.

C. He doesn't treat you as an equal. He stresses his superiority because he's "older," "smarter," "bigger," "stronger," "more experienced," "socially superior." He talks about women in general in negative terms. Pay particular attention to what he tells you about the women he has dated in the past. As I found out, to my personal detriment, it wasn't an accident that a man I was dating had five previous wives. He subscribed to the, "I am the king, you are the excrement on my shoe" theory of relationships. Men like this tip their hands early.

D. He mistreats you and other people physically by pushing, pulling, grabbing, hitting, pinning you down, and so forth. Even disguised as "play," this kind of behavior isn't fun. Also watch out if he becomes overly forceful when you are making out.

If he thinks that breaking down your resistance, or your boundaries, is okay when you're kissing, you may be sure that he will think it is okay to break down boundaries when it comes to penetration. Other warning signs include: cruelty to animals and children – people and pets who are weaker than he is. Pay particular attention if he's fascinated by weapons. A tip to men – nothing is more of a turn off than a man who grabs a woman's hand and plunks it on his penis. If your date isn't stroking you as you want to be stroked, she probably isn't ready and you shouldn't force the issue.

E. He tries to intimidate you by violating your personal, emotional or physical space. He sits too close, he uses his body to block your way, he touches you when you ask him not to, he stares you down, he gets physical (sexually or non-sexually) in ways that make you uncomfortable. If you don't like something he does, say so. If he continues to do it, in spite of what you say, take that as a warning and you might want to stop seeing him before he wants to engage in sexual intercourse.

F. He bosses you around. He tells you how to dress, he criticizes what you say, or how you behave, he tells you what you should and shouldn't do. He tells you who your friends should be. He criticizes your family and tries to isolate you from them. He flies off the handle at any frustration – particularly sexual. He is possessive and gets jealous for no apparent reason. No matter how attractive you find this man to be – watch out. A man who tries to separate you from your natural support is dangerous in the long run.

No matter how marvelous, attractive, appealing, stimulating and desirable these kinds of men appear to be, they will not turn out to have your best interest at heart. These are the profiles of men who become rapists or abusers. If one of them is pursuing you, identify him to your friends and avoid him. If he threatens you, stalks or abuses you, get proactive. Talk to the police or campus security immediately. Take his behavior very seriously.

3. **Don't Drink Alcohol If You Are Not Really Comfortable With Your Date.**

About 75% of men and 55% of women involved in date rape are under the influence of drugs or alcohol at the time of the rape. Women worry about date rape drugs – GHB, rohypnol, and ketamine, and they should be worried – but by far the worst culprit is alcohol, because it's legal, available and culturally acceptable – if not an actual peer pressure drink. Alcohol is also an entry point for the administration of date rape drugs. Drinking alcohol has several effects. It enhances men's aggressiveness while lowering their judgment. It lowers your intuition while lowering your judgment and your ability to defend yourself.

After a great deal of press about date rape drugs, one study of women who had themselves tested for date rape drugs, actually tested positive only for alcohol. This could be because date rape drugs do not stay in the system for longer than 72 hours. This could also be because they drank to excess and were negatively affected by their drinking to an extent they didn't believe possible for a legal and socially well accepted drug. Alcohol is not benign. It is very hard for the younger and less experienced drinker to know when enough is enough, since there is a delay in time between when you drink the alcohol and when it enters your bloodstream and begins to affect your mind and behavior.

When I worked as an EMT on an ambulance, we knew that Super Bowl Sunday would be the day we saw more instances of serious spousal abuse than any other day – even New Year's Eve. The reason was that Super Bowl Sunday was the day of heaviest drinking, and the day on which men were identified with aggressive sport. Drinking and aggressive sports are not a good mix. Like drinking and aggressive sports activities, and drinking and driving, drinking and dating are very bad combinations.

It is important for both men and women to know that if a woman has engaged in sex – but cannot remember doing it or consenting to it – the woman is considered to have been raped, whether drugs were used or not. Non-consensual sex is rape. So it isn't just on the other side of "No," it's also a requirement that the woman (or man) be capable of saying, "Yes." Capable includes being conscious, old enough and with a high enough IQ.

4. **Figuring out if you have fallen victim to a rape in which a date rape drug was used is difficult, but not impossible.**

First, there are some very clear signs that sexual activity has taken place, even if you have no memory of actually "doing it." Signs that a sexual assault has taken place can include:

* soreness or bruising in the genital area

* soreness or bruising in the anal area

* bruising on the inner and/or outer thighs

* bruising on the wrists and forearms

* defensive bruising or scratching

* traces of semen or vaginal fluids on clothes, body or nearby furniture

* used condoms near you or in nearby garbage containers

An extremely reliable sign of rape is gossip about what happened. Contrary to popular belief – men *do* talk. They brag and they have been known to exaggerate.

5. **Signs of Date Rape Drugs**

Indications of sexual activity aside, clues that a date rape drug may have been slipped into your drink come from the drugs themselves. People who have been given date rape drugs:

* appear to be very drunk, no matter how much or little they have had to drink,

* feel "hung-over," despite having ingested little or no alcohol,

* have a sense of having had hallucinations or very "real" dreams or fleeting memories of feeling or acting intoxicated, despite having taken no drugs or drinking no alcohol,

* have no clear memory of events during an 8 – 24-hour period, with no known reason for the memory lapse,

* hear stories from others about how intoxicated they seemed at a time when they knew they had taken no drugs, medications or alcohol,

* have sustained injuries to breasts, anus or vagina with no memory of how they could have been sustained.

Short of being told that you have been given a date rape drug, there is no way to be sure without medical testing. If you suspect that you have been given a date rape drug, you need to get to a hospital quickly and you must request that you be properly tested. The drugs can be found in your system if you act quickly. If you suspect that you have been raped using any one of these drugs, go to a hospital and request a preliminary rape exam which includes testing for date rape drugs. This is the only way to know for sure.

6. How do you protect yourself against date rape drugs?

Be paranoid. Travel in packs and watch each other's backs. Be proactive. I have not used drugs or alcohol since I was 21 and I realized I could not handle substances. At my husband's best friend's house one night, the "friend" decided to lace my soda with alcohol because he didn't believe I was serious about not drinking. I tasted it immediately, was incredibly nasty to him and poured it out. After that I never accepted a drink (including water) from that man again. Luckily for me it was an alcohol which I could taste. I would not have been able to taste a date rape drug.

Here are some rules for protecting yourself from being drugged:

* Don't accept open drinks (alcoholic or non-alcoholic in glasses or cans and bottles that have been opened by someone else out of your site) from anyone you don't implicitly trust which is no one except yourself.

* When in bars or clubs, always get your drink *directly* from the bartender and be sure not to take your eyes off the bartender or your order at any time. Don't order from a waiter or waitress or let somebody go to the bar for you

* At parties, only accept drinks in closed containers: bottles, cans or tetra packs. Open them yourself.

* Never leave your drink unattended or even turn your back on your table. If you don't finish your drink before you dance, make sure to get a fresh drink when you return to your table. So what if the drinks are expensive.

* Do not drink from open beverage sources like punch bowls, pitchers or tubs, which may have already been drugged.

* Keep your eyes and ears open; if there is talk of date rape drugs or if friends seem "too intoxicated" compared to the amount they have imbibed, leave the party or club immediately and don't go back – and if you are a true friend – take your friend with you!

If these behavior modifications don't feel like enough protection, or if you don't think you can follow these rules on a given night, you do have another option. There is a brand new defense against date rape drugs that has recently been approved for use in North America; it is a simple and inexpensive test kit that you can use to detect the presence of date rape drugs in drinks.

This "**Drink Safe Technology**" is a package of drink testing strips or coasters that work like litmus paper strips you use to test for pH balance in Chemistry class. These strips or coasters change color when they come in contact with a date rape drug. The strips fit in your purse or pocket and can be used quickly and discretely.

To find out more about "**Drink Safe,**" visit the website at www.drinksafetech.com[6].

Other Ways To Protect Yourself When Dating.

1. Learn how to say, "No," and mean it.

In American culture, in books, magazines, TV shows and movies, the cultural stereotype for the desirable woman is the submissive doormat. We are trained to be compliant. Women who assert themselves are often called, "bitches" and aspersions are cast on their sexual preferences. Rush Limbaugh called Sandra Fluke a slut for wanting to testify in front of Congress in favor of birth control. He suggested that Hilary Clinton was a lesbian for being a strong and powerful woman. He definitely would be one of those men who would fit into a "Rape Type" the one who continually demeans the women around him. And, he is definitely not alone in this line of name calling.

---

[6] http://www.drinksafetech.com/

No matter how that name-calling feels, it's better to be called a "bitch," "lesbian" or "dike" than to be raped. Don't buy into worrying about that stereotype. Don't worry about being disliked or rejected because you assert yourself. You have every right to say what, you want and don't want to participate in within every relationship. You don't owe anyone anything for spending money on you or for showing you a good time. Most particularly you don't have to go all the way with anyone simply because you started necking with them. You aren't responsible for satisfying your date – who is perfectly capable of satisfying himself if push comes to shove. If he tells you that he's hurting because you turned him on – you can remind him that driving in a car on a bumpy road probably gives him the same pain in the groin.

Don't be afraid to be assertive. Don't waver. Say no with your actions, as well as your words. If things begin to get out of control, stop what you're doing, look him in the eye and say, "No. I don't want to do this. Stop now." Or "Take me home now." Be prepared to walk home. Never leave home without money for a taxi and without comfortable shoes. Make sure your cell phone is charged and in your purse or pocket.

If you do say, "No," don't confuse the issue by kissing him, or stroking him, to make up or apologize. You don't help him by muddying the waters, and you put yourself at serious risk of not being believed. One thing that aggressive men enjoy is "making up" after a fight. Don't mislead your date into thinking that you are playing his game of resisting, so you can make up later. You'll find it much more difficult to stop him the second time around.

If your date persists in violating your boundaries, get out of the situation immediately. Does this sound a little like if you get raped it's your fault for not being assertive enough? It's not. What I'm saying is that you don't want to be raped and you have to do everything in your power to avert it. And even when you do, there is still a chance you can't prevent it.

2. Avoid being alone, particularly on his turf.

"Parking" is the activity most strongly associated with sexual aggression. When you spend a lot of time with a man necking in his car, in his apartment, in your apartment, in isolated areas like parks or the beach – particularly at night – an aggressive man can take that as, "asking for it." The aggressive man can lead himself to believe that if you are willing to be alone with him, you are as interested in sexual intercourse as he is. Again, be proactive – eliminate the possibility of misunderstanding by encouraging double dates and group activities. For a moment, let's give him the benefit of the doubt and say that your behavior is confusing – if you care for him then you want to protect him from himself. Date rape is a felony and it's the quickest way I know of to break up a nice relationship – short of finding the man unattractive.

Set a curfew for yourself. Make sure your date knows you are expected at home by a certain time. Make the time frame realistic so that you have enough time to have a soda, talk awhile, and drive home. It sets the boundary of unlimited parking. Most important, don't allow a violation of that time frame. When I was raped my grandparents had set a curfew. When the lifeguard turned onto the golf course it was a violation of that curfew. I firmly believe that if I had spoken up in that moment and said "I have to be home in five minutes," the rape would have been avoided. He would have known I was not "asking for it." Once you have shown that a curfew is a relative term, everything else you say can become immediately relative.

3. Don't send unintentional messages.

No matter how innocent your intentions are if you play into the myths that men have about women, you may be courting trouble. Dress conservatively. Men have been known to use miniskirts, exposed navels or cleavage as a justification for rape. Call conservative dressing and acting a reinforcement of your decision not to have sex. Men get aroused most often by what they see. Sex is probably number one on a man's mind when he's around women, or even thinking about being around women. As I have mentioned before, aggressive men use almost any excuse to justify their behavior. It's up to you to provide as little justification as possible even if you feel a little weird about being so conservative.

Does that sound wrong? Is it unfair that you have to be on your guard all the time? Well, life's unfair. Floods, earthquakes, hurricanes, car accidents, and rapes happen to good and innocent people. If you are at risk of something bad happening, you generally take precautions to mitigate the risk – so this is just like not building your house on a fault line or in a flood plain, or speeding on the wrong side of the road – live defensively and don't ask for trouble you don't want.

4. Avoid blind dates.

Or, if you are going to go on a blind date, make it a double date or invite him to join your pack. Let the man you are dating get to know you as a person. And, get to know him. Once he knows you, he is less likely to view you as merely a sex object (less likely, not unlikely). And you have to give yourself time to know whether he's the kind of man you actually want to date, or if he's really someone you want to avoid. It's harder to keep the masks on over time. So get to see who your date really is before you expose yourself to the risks of being alone with him.

5. *TRUST YOUR INSTINCTS!*

I used to think I didn't have instincts. At some point I realized I had them, but I wasn't in the habit of listening to them. As I told you earlier, I intercepted a look between my date rapist's, two friends that should have warned me not to go out with him. I wondered about the look when I saw it, but I didn't listen to that small warning voice. We all have instincts. We all have small warning voices. Don't override them. LISTEN, and then act on them. Better foolish than sorry.

But, you say, I might miss out on a great time. Better to miss out than be raped. That doesn't mean avoid all dates and all men for all time – it means *listen* when you have a *feeling* that something isn't quite right and act preventively on that feeling. Don't turn your personal power over to someone else.

To quote a woman I met at a bus stop in New York City one day, "Never run for a bus or a man, there will be another one along in only five minutes." It might surprise you to know that "Soul Mates" are a dime a dozen.

6. Take precautions at all times.

I remember giving an unusual test on CPR to a cross section of people who lived and worked in my town. I described a scene in which someone keeled over while eating a donut at the dining room table and asked those taking the test what they would do. 92% did the wrong thing. Next, I asked them why they had chosen to do whatever it was they did, every one of them said, "It's common sense, isn't it?" It was at that point that I fully understood that common sense should never be equated with knowledge or training. Educate yourself to the ways in which to protect yourself. Never rely on "common sense."

* If you find yourself in a rape situation and there are people around, don't bother to yell for help. Yell, "Fire." Tests show that people are less likely to respond to calls for help, which presents an unknown hazard to them, than they are to calls for fire, which they immediately know can endanger them so they run toward the calls for fire to help put it out. If you happen to be alone in the street with the rapist, at the least you get people in nearby buildings to run outside.

* Do not give your address or telephone number to anyone you don't know well. If you want to see an excellent example of how people with mal intent get information from you, watch the telephone scene in the movie _Déjà Vu_. It's a great cautionary moment.

* In the same vein, don't volunteer information about yourself on the phone. Never tell anyone you are alone unless you know them very well.

* Keep your curtains and blinds drawn at night and in the early morning. Keep the lights on inside and have the capacity to light the outside as well. Outside lights that automatically sense the approach of people are very much advised.

* If you suspect a prowler, turn on all the outside lights, call the police and alert your neighbors. Do not go running out of your house to see who's there. The police would much rather respond to a false alarm than to the report of a victim of a crime.

* Never open the door if you are not certain of the person on the other side. From personal experience, I once opened the door to my landlord who was drunk out of his mind and had come to the conclusion that I was hiding the wife he had been beating. I foolishly opened the door, because first, I didn't realize the condition he was in, and then wasn't strong enough to get the door closed again.

Fortunately, she wasn't hiding in my apartment and when he couldn't find her he didn't turn on me.

* If someone claiming to be from the Gas Company, Electric Company, Cable Company or Phone Company knocks on your door without an appointment – don't let them in. Call their company immediately to ascertain whether they have been sent to your house. Chances are, they are not from the company and you should call the Police. At the very least, look outside to see if their company truck is parked within view.

* Chain locks are a joke. One quick kick and they're history. Use deadbolt locks on your doors. Lock all doors and windows when you are away. If you have windows in your doors be sure your deadbolts can only be opened with a key and never leave the key in the lock. Be particularly careful to lock windows that have access from the ground floor or fire escapes. Better a hot apartment than a dangerous intruder.

* Keep your car doors locked and windows rolled up when you drive in traffic. In your neighborhood, learn where the nearest fire stations or police stations are located. If you think that someone is following you, don't drive home, drive to the police station or firehouse and honk your horn until you attract someone's attention.

* If your car breaks down or runs out of gas, raise the hood, then get back inside the car, lock the doors, call 911 on your cell and wait for the police. If ANYONE stops to offer you help, stay in your car and don't roll down the windows. They can call for help if they have a cell and you don't.

* If you are a woman alone in a vehicle, don't stop to help someone by the side of the road. Use your cell phone to report the problem. There have been recent reports of people being robbed and beaten when they have stopped to help someone by the side of the road. If you see another woman in distress by the side of the road, don't stop to help. Call 911 – get the license number of the car. We live in dangerous times and it is advisable to act as if every situation has the potential to be hazardous.

* Never pick up hitchhikers – male or female.

* Never hitchhike or take rides from strangers. Two of my three children got into serious trouble hitchhiking. Fortunately, they also got out of it without more than being so thoroughly frightened. They never thumbed a ride again.

* Always lock your car when you leave it, even for a short time. Make that a habit so you don't forget. You may occasionally lock your keys in the car, but that is much better than getting raped. If possible,

park in a brightly lit spot. If the lights are out for any reason, think twice about parking there.

* When walking, stick to well-populated areas. Don't walk alone if you can avoid it. When I attended the University of Vermont, the part of the road between the girl's dorms and the main campus was hazardous if you were alone.

* If you are the recipient of an obscene phone call, hang up immediately. Life has become harder for the obscene caller with the advent of Caller ID. Protect yourself and don't answer calls from people whose number you don't know – they can leave messages and you can call back. Or block calls from unidentified callers. It costs more, but it certainly discourages obscenity from strangers.

* If you are uncomfortable with a phone conversation, even with someone you know very well, say so. You don't have to tolerate someone using you for their sexual pleasure on the phone. Don't even bother with gently changing the subject. Tell whoever it is you don't like the conversation. Men cannot read your mind and you don't have to beat around the bush. If the man refuses to change the subject, he's probably someone you want to avoid. Phone sex, like all sex, should be consensual.

* Listen to your friends. The jungle drums of gossip about the reality of the men around you are not

fantasies. If you hear something negative, don't discount it simply because you like the man or you're not sure if you like the gossip. If you decide to see someone in spite of what your friends say about him, be smart about where you're going and how you're going to get there.

* Don't be concerned about offending your date by being up front and firm. If he gets angry about a decision you make about going somewhere with him, or stopping what he's doing physically because it goes beyond your boundaries or comfort zone – this is probably the kind of man you may be inclined to ignore you when you say, "no," or "stop." Rapists can be charming, delightful, handsome, appealing, warm, friendly, intelligent and funny. They don't wear signs on their foreheads. They do, however, clearly exhibit certain identifiable personality traits that announce their intentions. It's up to you to protect yourself.

6. Verbalizing your appreciation for the man who respects you doesn't mean letting down your guard.

When you date someone who is kind, considerate and respectful, acknowledge that. Men love to hear nice things about themselves as much as you do. That does not mean letting down your guard or doing something that is beyond your comfort zone simply because he asks nicely.

Chapter 6

Guidelines for Men

This book isn't just about the repercussions of rape or abuse on men and women who are the victims of this heinous crime. This book is a warning to rapists and would-be rapists as well.

Guidelines for men come in two flavors. One is for the men who are dating women, one is for men who are dating men. Every warning for the women being dated applies to men who are being dated. 10% of date rapes are man to man.

If you rape someone, it can mean the end of your productive life. Felony convictions generally don't have happy endings. Jail time doesn't lead to the corner office with the big windows. A moment's pleasure can mean a lifetime of misery – so think about whether abusing someone else is really worth the damage you do to them and the potential for a very bad outcome for you. Unfortunately, in our present court system there are outcomes that are predicated on how rich a rapist is. We have to do something about that. Meanwhile those of you who aren't billionaires had better pay attention to the justice system that affects the other 99%.

1. **Understand, it is never okay to force anyone to have sex.**

No matter how much money you spend on her, no matter how far she's let you go, no matter if you are in bed and naked – if she says "no" – stop. Actually, if she doesn't say "yes," stop. No matter what your friends tell you, no matter how many other men you think she has had, no matter what – non-consensual sex is a felony.

2. "No," isn't the only thing you have to worry about.

There are a list of extenuating circumstances that can turn you into a felon. Diminished capacity comes in three flavors:

* competence to make the decision (is she drunk, drugged or unconscious).

* diminished mental capacity to make the decision (Is her IQ too low to make an informed decision) – or

* age (is she too young to make the decision).

Remember that rape is non-consensual sex. Statutory rape is still regarded as non-consensual and a felony, even with an eagerly consenting teenager. The law recognizes that children, men and women below a certain IQ, or those who are unconscious, do not have the ability to consent. And, ignorance is no excuse under the law. The point is, know who you're dating and don't make a mistake that can cost you your own quality of life.

3. Respect her limits.

Girls in women's bodies can be deceptive. They look hot, they may dress or dance hot, but they may not *be* hot. If you run into limits you weren't expecting because she acts as if "she wants it," pay attention. You cannot read anyone's mind. Unless she actually *asks* for it, she isn't asking for it. If's she's not allowed by law to ask for it, she's not asking for it. And if she isn't asking for it, don't do it. You may be way more experienced than she is. It is not your job to push her limits. It isn't your job to be her teacher against her will. Some of the things you think would be fun, would be frankly horrifying to an inexperienced lover.

4. Read the stereotypes of the dominant, aggressive male and choose a different way to act.

The attitudes, "I am the king," "Act first, think later" and "Who Cares About You," created the myths around women that have lead to 1 in 8 college men raping their dates. Don't believe those stereotypes. Treat the women you are dating the way you would want a young man to treat your mother, your sister or your daughter. Give them love and respect and the rewards will be amazing.

One of the great myths about men is that they are animals who don't have any control over their urges. That's an excuse for bad behavior, and it isn't real. All men have control of themselves, unless they're drinking or using drugs like PHP. Being unable to control your urges isn't an excuse under the law, and it shouldn't be a reason for you to get out of line with your date.

5. Don't drink and date.

If you have trouble with alcohol – and you should quickly discover if you do – then don't drink. I discovered that I couldn't hold my liquor when I was 21. I decided at that point that I simply didn't want to be an alcoholic like the rest of the women in my family. I stopped drinking then and consider it to have been the best decision I have ever made. Alcohol is the worst drug in the world. It's made even worse by its social acceptability and accessibility. Know yourself, know your limits, and be in control of your actions. It's your life. I know that all kinds of politicians, celebrities and religious leaders use the, "I am an alcoholic" defense when they get caught doing things they shouldn't. Alcoholism isn't a defense, it's a preventable disease. Like smoking, it's better not to start it than to struggle with stopping it.

6. Never Administer Date Rape Drugs

My freshman year in college my very steady boy friend suffered an epileptic seizure while driving my car. Fortunately we had pulled over at the time. We had been dating intensely for four months and this was the first I knew about his seizure disorder. Not only was he too embarrassed to tell be about it. He had stopped taking his medication to "cure" himself of the problem so we could get married without his having to ever tell me about it. The point of that story is to warn you that epileptics are often very reluctant to share the fact with friends and dates. Over my years on ambulances as an EMT and Paramedic I would respond to calls for seizures and the person who had just had a grand mal seizure would swear she didn't have a problem. Of course the medication in their purse or pocket said otherwise. It is quite possible that she might not even have taken her meds for fear of having to explain her condition to the friends she was with – who did not know about the problem either.

The point of these little cautionary tales is not about fessing up to the truth. It's about how embarrassing people with conditions like epilepsy find that problem to be. They take very strong prescription drugs that can have very serious interactions with date rape drugs. Even if you know a woman fairly well or even very well you might not know that she is taking prescription medications that will not mix well with the drugs you are secretly administering – interactions that could prove fatal. Think about trying to explain to a jury that you didn't know your date was on another drug when the drug you were intending to administer in secret was designed to make her pass out so she wouldn't remember being raped by you – it really wasn't your fault because she hadn't informed you that she was already taking drugs…that might create a degree of lack of sympathy when it comes to jail time – don't you think?

Chapter 7

What do you do when you're being raped?

Suppose you've taken precautions. Suppose you are certain your date is one of the good guys. Suppose, in spite of everything you do, you do get raped. Rape experts suggest:

1. Remain calm.

Surveys suggest that women who managed to avoid being raped had a more controlled emotional response to the initial attack. You need to be able to think. Keeping down the fear, blame and powerlessness helps you keep yourself from panicking and allows you to concentrate on being assertive.

2. Act quickly.

Don't give your attacker time to gain momentum. Don't deceive yourself for a second that things will get better if you reason with him. If he hasn't stopped at this point, he's not suddenly going to turn back into your friend. He has become, for whatever reason, a predator capable of raping you, hurting you and even killing you. Decide on a plan of action and get moving.

3. Run away, if possible.

Get out of his grasp and run for help. Run toward lights and people, run toward buildings and the street. You need to get among people. If you are in a car, get out. If you can't get out and you can use the horn, without jeopardizing yourself further, use it.

4. Scream FIRE.

If you can't get away, scream. Your scream will immediately alert people nearby that you are in trouble. Don't bother to scream, "Help!" Many people won't help if they think helping will put them in jeopardy. Scream "Fire!" Fire will put them in physical jeopardy, so they'll act immediately. They will run from their house and your rapist will be exposed for what he is doing. They may think they can put the fire out, so they'll run toward your voice instead of away from you. Best of all, screaming "Fire" may surprise your attacker and give you precious seconds to get free and run.

5. Attack.

I am a great supporter of Karate for women. If you can, look for a way to hurt him physically. If he has already exposed his genitals, hurt them. Grab, kick them or hit them as hard as you possibly can. Make your best shot your first shot because there is a real possibility that your attack will generate further violence. The problem for most of us is that the very idea of kicking someone in the balls, or gouging their eyes, or hurting them in any other way, is so foreign as to be almost impossible to consider, even under duress. That's why it's such a good idea to study the martial arts. Train yourself to do the things you normally wouldn't do. Here's a warning: If you don't feel you can hurt him, it's probably not a good idea to try.

6. Buy Time.

If it looks like you can't attract attention, try to talk your attacker out of his actions. Get very cold in your body, very stern, very strong. Tell him that his behavior is completely out of line. Ask him what he'd do if someone did this to his sister or his mother. Ask him what his father will think of him or his friends. If he relaxes his guard, try to escape. Don't threaten with publicity – it might make him want to silence you. Tell him you're a lesbian and you find him repulsive. That worked for me once when a man I knew quite well offered me a ride home.

7. If your life is threatened.

If you think your life is threatened, or if you simply are not strong enough to get away, you may have to give in.

Giving in does not mean that you consented to being raped, it means that you are saving yourself from further harm. It is no less a rape if you give in than if you resist until you get seriously hurt or killed. If you are raped, it is not your fault. You are not to blame. Most of all, your soul isn't touched by the rape – only your body. If you are raped, take action as soon as possible.

Chapter 8

What Do I Do If I Have Been Raped?

The first thing to do after you have been raped is to get immediately proactive. So many men and women who have experienced rape continue to be raped in their minds for years after the event. It's such a betrayal that it's difficult to get beyond it. So many emotions run wild after something this traumatic: guilt, shame, embarrassment, humiliation, betrayal, disbelief, self-blame, powerlessness, denial, fear, anxiety and rage. There's even a name for it – Rape Trauma Syndrome.

Let's get clear what happened – we are talking about date rape in this case. A man you trusted with your safety and well-being – perhaps a man you loved – had sexual intercourse with you against your will. He may have gotten violent and brutal with you as well. You must understand that any emotions connected to that rape are completely normal. You are not isolated or alone because of that experience. One in eight college women have bee raped and one in four have been sexually abused. Most importantly, however, it's important to know that all the horrible feelings, fears and concerns do not have to last forever.

Physical Responses to Date Rape

For many victims of date rape, male or female, the first, most notable, sign of rape is physical discomfort. This isn't a rule, so it may not apply to you at all. Some victims report that their body is "sore all over." Others say that their genitalia are sore, or their anus hurts because of the force their assailant used. Sometimes the sore areas are the neck, throat, chest or ribs. Sometimes the assailant has hit them in the mouth and loosened teeth, or they have suffered bruises and abrasions trying to escape.

Another common symptom of rape is loss of sleep. Again, this isn't a rule. Some victims report that they have difficulty falling asleep, or sometimes wake up because of nightmares and then they can't get back to sleep. Other victims lose their appetite, or they start to binge in an effort to "stuff" their feelings. All kinds of eating disorders can be laid at the feet of sexual abuse or rape, including bulimia (binging and then throwing up), and anorexia (self-starvation).

Other rape-related compulsive behaviors include compulsive exercising, perfectionism, housecleaning, over-achieving, drug abuse, alcohol abuse and even sex abuse – as if one rape weren't enough.

A number of women have talked about hating their body, as if their body was responsible for the assault. And they punish that body with unhealthy behaviors of all kinds. The rape was the fault of the rapist, not the victim, not the victim's body, but the victim pays and continues to pay.

If you are a man reading this book, remember that rape isn't innocent, that it always has tremendous consequences for the victim and it is *NEVER* the victim's fault.

Emotional Responses to Date Rape

There are any number of emotional responses that accompany date rape and you may experience any, all or none of them – there are no rules. The emotional responses to acquaintance rape are so varied and numerous that I might miss a couple of them. Also, there's no order to these feelings. Each of us experiences a trauma like this differently.

1. **The first great emotional feeling is that of loss and betrayal**.

You trusted the rapist and he betrayed you and you might feel as if you can never trust anyone ever again. There are so many complicated feelings of loss involving rape: loss of self-respect, loss of trust, loss of self-esteem, loss of feeling valuable as a woman, perhaps loss of virginity. Take some time to actually grieve for your losses. This violation is a form of emotional death – death of innocence, death of trust – and should be acknowledged. It's hard to get beyond something you don't accept.

The thing is that you can have all these feelings without being raped. Simply coping with a man's unwanted sexual attentions brings up all those emotions. There are a million ways to feel violated by men that don't involve rape. The problem with being raped is that you think these negative or self-loathing emotions justified. The truth is they aren't. You didn't do anything wrong. Even if you dressed in a min-skirt up to your naval and drank until you passed out, it's not your fault. No matter what anyone tells you – particularly the rapist – you aren't responsible for being raped or sexually assaulted. You are not responsible for his behavior EVER. Pushing you beyond your consent is the rapist's responsibility. Period.

Because so much of your belief in yourself has been undermined, it's important to take immediate steps to make certain that the rapist is brought to justice. Taking action against someone you may have cared about may not seem like a "nice" thing for you to do, but it means that the rapist won't feel free to rape again. It is important to send the message to men who think that pushing their sexual desires on women is permissible that it's not okay. Justice and accountability are action steps. It is important that you take action and stay in action. And if you can't, that's okay too.

2. The second great emotional feeling is that of guilt.

The great majority of women who have been raped feel emotionally responsible for complicity in the crime. And the matter is made much worse by the rapist's insistence that they are complicit. Women will run a list of *"if onlys"* through their minds. The lists are parallel with the list of blame that the rapist is perpetrating – and they're both part of the great rape myth. *"If only I hadn't worn that short skirt," "If only I hadn't gone to his room," "If only I had insisted we stay with the group," "If only I hadn't flirted with him,"* and on and on and on. Here's the point – you can *"if only"* yourself to death and the rape still won't be your fault. You didn't cause the rape, you didn't rape yourself, and rape is never your fault.

This isn't about a woman's behavior. This is about a man's behavior. You may have been charming and flirtatious, you may even have thought you wanted to have sex with him, you may have had sex with him in the past, you may have utterly compromised yourself in being alone, being sexually aroused with him, but the point is, the minute you said, "no," his obligation was to stop. If you couldn't say, "no," because of drugs or alcohol, his obligation was to stop.

The strangest thing about guilt and rape is that simply being involved in something so wrong brings up feelings of guilt in the innocent party. Women who are victims of rape are not accessories before, during or after the fact. No matter how the rapist tries to shift the blame, you are the victim, not the accessory, and the rape was not your fault.

Society isn't helpful either. "She must have done something to lead him on," is a prevalent belief. It is necessary for a rapist's legal defense team to make certain to blame the victim because they have a responsibility to defend their client, but that doesn't mean that the rapist isn't guilty or that the victim is not innocent. For years, women didn't bring rapists to court because the courts and the law didn't support or protect them. Things are a little better now, although in recent years there has been a degree of backsliding, but there is still an overriding belief that victims are the real perpetrators of rape. "Nice girls don't get raped," is an erroneous statement uttered by men and women, and it's completely false. Nice girls do get raped all the time and it is never their fault.

The very real point is that nothing you did, short of not dating, would have prevented what happened to you – and the kicker is that not dating is not a guarantee either. Men who rape are men who justify their behavior by whatever means they can. They will find as many people as they can to get into agreement with them so they feel better about what they did. That doesn't change anything. They raped you and it's not your fault.

3. The third great emotional consequence is denial.

Because it's so hard to believe that someone you know would actually rape you, you will justify his behavior as "not rape." He couldn't have raped you because he loves you. He couldn't abuse you because he loves you and because he loves you, he must be right that you really wanted it. He couldn't have raped you, and therefore you must have been cooperating on some level. He couldn't have raped you because he says he loves you so much, so on some level you must have been complicit. The emotions surrounding the rape get overridden, buried, silenced and never healed. Even worse, the rapist never gets the message that his behavior is not okay and has consequences, and other women are never warned. One of several things will happen. You will continue to date, or even marry, the rapist and leave yourself open for continued violation and increasing abuse – because of course, it's not his fault, and even if you don't want to have intercourse with him, it isn't really rape because he loves you – doesn't he? Or, you and your rapist will stop dating and he will do the same thing to someone else.

One of the reasons that 1 in 8 girls in college get raped is because of this pattern of denial. A victim can't believe that it was really rape and doesn't talk about it. So you never hear that it happened to your friends or someone else on campus. It's too humiliating, it's too embarrassing to discuss with anyone. As a result, the rapist continues raping or abusing. And the victim keeps being wounded by the damage that the betrayal did to her self-confidence, her ability to trust herself.

The most important and healing thing the victim of rape can do is report the rape. Make certain that the rapist is stopped. Stop the denial. Seek help. Get him help. Get active in making certain that the rapist doesn't think that what he's doing is permissible so he continues to do it.

Here's a rule: Rape is never an act of love.

4. Number four is fear.

Women who have been raped do not trust themselves and their judgment. They do not trust men. They fear living alone or even being alone. Any trigger that she associates with the man who raped her – smell, size, body type, body hair, can result in a fear response from the woman.

41% of rape victims expect to be raped again. And, without help they may be right. Many women fear being raped by the same man again, and in many cases they are right.

Fear of repeated rape may lead to self-protection like self-defense courses, changing phone numbers, adding door locks and window bars, getting a roommate, sleeping with the light on – but many rape victims don't change their minds about being a victim. It is very important to address fear where it exists – in your mind. Without addressing the fear caused by rape, women can be scarred for life. It's not fair and it's fixable.

5. Number five is lowered self-esteem.

Many rape victims feel there must be something wrong with them because their date didn't respect them enough not to rape them. They see themselves as lowered in value because they have become "damaged goods." The statistics bear this one out. In a recent study, 82% of the women interviewed said that the experience had changed them. 30% contemplated suicide and 31% had sought out psychotherapy to deal with the repercussions.

It's actually normal to have a sense of hopelessness or worthlessness following a rape. It goes hand-in-hand with the abuse, violation and betrayal that is rape. It may be a normal feeling, but it's not a feeling that should be allowed to continue. That's why it's so important to place the blame where it belongs – on the head of the man who committed the crime. You said no. You expected to be listened to. That fact that you were betrayed does not mean there's something wrong with you. It means there is something wrong with the man in whom you put your trust. And don't think that it's always easy to know when a man isn't to be trusted. The great serial murderers of our times were charming, handsome, and inspired trust in their victims.

If you are having trouble coping with being a rape victim, don't wait and let the problem fester. Seek competent help immediately. Contrary to popular belief, there is a lot of counseling available. If you are in school, immediately seek counseling through the school. Those with limited funds who are not in school can look to their church, the United Way, the YMCA, local hospitals, university psychology departments and graduate school counseling departments. Other organizations include the National Alliance on Mental Illness (nami.org), Recover, Inc. (recovery-inc.org), The American Association of Pastoral Counselors (aapc.org) and Samaritan Counseling Centers (samaritaninstitute.org).

Chapter 9

The Big Question:
How Can I Survive Date Rape?

It's so easy to second-guess the decisions that lead to date rape. As the saying goes "Hindsight is always 20-20." Victims of rape spend their time reconstructing the past and beating themselves up about precautions they didn't take. Perpetrators of rape, if they do think about their behavior, spend their time justifying their actions and trying to get their friends to agree that what they did was right.

No matter what happened, you can't undo it, and self-punishment is not the correct way to handle it. If you allow the rape to continue in your mind, you will deprive yourself of the quality of life you so richly deserve. Putting the rape behind you and learning how to avoid rape in the future is what is required for healing. The absolutely most healing thing that you can do is get into action on your own behalf.

Steps To Take Immediately After A Rape Occurs

There are a number of steps that you should take immediately after you've been raped. Back at the time when I was raped, women who were raped were generally considered to have been the perpetrator. There was no support system in place and my family was not exactly a group you would go to with a problem like that. My sister, who I do trust on that level, was a teenager. Fortunately, AIDS wasn't rampant at the time, and I didn't get pregnant – which contrary to common belief in the conservative world happens quite frequently.

Like 42% of rape victims, I told no one about what had happened. I buried the incident and went on to face propositions, groping, and all kinds of unwanted, even threatening, attention from acquaintances and strangers for years.

Today, things are somewhat different. There is support, although I think you have to be proactive in accessing it. At least now recognized that rape is never the victim's fault. However, there are things that are available for you to do immediately and over the long term.

Immediately:

1. Tell Someone You Trust About What Happened.

You really do need support from someone you know well, who will stand with you as you deal with the days following the rape. It could be a family member, a school counselor or a close friend, be careful who you choose because not everyone is great at support, but choose someone and tell them what happened right away. If you don't know someone you trust on that level, get on line and contact the Rape, Abuse & Incest National Network (www.rainn.org). This is the largest organization of its kind and operates a rape hotline 24/7.

There are many reasons why date or acquaintance rape victims fail to tell someone what happened. The number one reason is that even if they have said, "No," they feel complicit on some level and don't feel that what happened to them could actually have been rape. Some women are afraid of their rapist and fear retaliation if they tell. Women still believe that if they tell someone about being raped, other people will think they are bad on some level – that if they hadn't been "bad" they could have avoided the problem. Some women just want to avoid the hassle that dealing with rape will cause, and some are convinced that no one will believe them.

However, burying a rape can result in severe psychological and emotional consequences. Not dealing with the aftermath of rape can lead to years of fear, anger and mistrust. It can lead to substance abuse, overeating to "self medicate" or "self-protecting" and to suppressing feelings. Overeating can lead to obesity and a panoply of fat-related diseases. And, it can lead to a string of broken relationships and in the worst case, suicide.

Get help. Tell someone. Get support. Have a reality check. Tell someone at the rape hotline what happened. Let an expert help you decide if what happened was rape in case you're not quite sure. Objectivity is a great support in this case.

2. Seek Medical Attention.

If the rape was violent – if you struggled hard – you may have sustained physical injury of which you are not immediately aware. This is why it's important to get help right away. Additionally, there is the possibility of sexually transmitted disease or pregnancy that you want to protect against. Ask a friend, call an ambulance, or take yourself to an emergency room, urgent care facility or your personal physician for a checkup. Do it right away, as date rape drugs have a short life in your body and morning after pills are available to handle the pregnancy issue.

Now, you may feel dirty because of the rape and it may be embarrassing to have a vaginal examination, particularly after you've had sexual intercourse, but don't take a shower or douche before you see the doctor. Valuable evidence of the rape, which will confirm the identity of your attacker, like public hair or DNA, could be lost if you wash it away. Additionally, many sexually transmitted diseases can be identified from the semen of your attacker – so for your protection, don't wash the evidence off.

3. Decide About Reporting The Rape To The Police.

Sometimes deciding to report a rape is easy. You don't know the man very well, he seriously injured you, you don't like him and never did… that's an easy report. Sometimes reporting the rape is much less easy. He's your boyfriend, you have loved him and thought you were going to marry him… He's your husband or the father of your children…He's your uncle, your stepfather… those are much more difficult reports. Reporting the rape will probably result in an investigation, arrest and legal proceedings that will involve you and the man who raped you facing off in court. Here are a million reasons why rape victims don't press charges against people who rape them. There are a couple of reasons why you should press charges. The most important reason is to prevent the rapist from raping someone else. We've talked about this before – men who think that rape is all right, don't hesitate to rape again. Women who forgive, try to forget and marry their rapist end up dealing with forced sex inside their marriage. It is very important to stop the rapist right at the beginning. If there are never any repercussions for bad behavior why should the perpetrator of a violent crime stop? Having said that, reporting a rape is a judgment call and ultimately you have to do what works for you.

Long Term:

1…If you haven't done steps one to three above, then it's time to simply face what happened.

In short, don't do what I did, do what I say. Burying the problem can lead to self-destructive behaviors. You may not know why you're overeating, or why you have stopped dating or going to parties, you just do it. Your subconscious is very powerful and the only way you can know what's going on inside that part of your mind is through the results in your behavior. You don't want to be dominated by the rape so that it becomes part of your identity ("I am a rape survivor"), at the same time, you do want to be able to talk about it.

2. Find A Safe Place And Take Time To Recuperate.

Whether you stay with a friend or with your family, take time to get some perspective on what happened. You may need to heal physically, but even if you don't, take time to recover emotionally. As I said before, in both the great traumas of my college life – getting raped and the death of my father which happened within months of each other – I took no time to recover. I plunged back into school activities as if nothing had happened, buried my feelings and didn't deal with any of them for years. Only recurrent nightmares let me know that I hadn't dealt with them If possible, share recovery time with someone you trust, who you can talk to in complete safety. Experience all those feelings of rage, violation, powerlessness and vulnerability in a safe space.

Recovering from rape is a mourning process – mourning for innocence and for trust, for the days when you believed in your own ability to judge the men you selected to date. You have to give yourself the time, space and comfort to get over the betrayal and to revive your self-esteem and self-respect. Even if you don't buy into the myth that it's your fault, rape still leaves you with a feeling that you made a mistake in judgment.

A really helpful tool is a journal. As a writer, I always write when I want to understand something better. Slowing your thoughts down to the speed of writing very often brings you answers that simple thinking overlooks. There is a marvelous tool called "The Non-dominant Hand Process," that not only slows your thinking still further, but also gives you unexpected answers to deal with problems. Using the hand you usually write with, simply write a question like: "What do I need to know about what happened to me last night?" Then shift your pen to the hand you usually don't use for writing and you should get some answers. You can ask, "What do I need to do in order to come to terms with what happened?" or "What do I need to do to avoid this again?" Keep asking questions with your dominant hand. Answer them with your non-dominant hand, and let the answers come. You don't have to act on the answers, unless you want to, but they're a great exploration of your feelings and intuition. You can also use this technique to examine any changes you are experiencing in your behaviors, so that you can stop them before they dominate your life. A good question is, "What can I do to trust again?" or "What can I do to restore my self-respect?

3. Seek Counseling.

It's a good idea to talk to a professional, someone who will neither make you wrong, nor inflame the drama of the situation making it more difficult to heal. You can, of course, heal without professional help – it's just helpful to have it. Again, the people at the rape hotline can refer you to people who are experienced in dealing with the aftermath of rape. Talking through what happened to you with a neutral person can be a vital step on the road to recovery.

4. Make Certain You Know Who's Guilty In This Circumstance.

The sub title of this book is, "It's Not Your Fault." Make certain that you don't fall into the trap of taking on the responsibility for what happened to you. The victim is never responsible for being raped. The rapist is guilty. There is no argument with that – being raped is never your fault.

5. Confront Your Rapist.

If you choose not to report your rapist to the police, you should still not let your rapist off the hook – and that's not always easy. The confrontation, because it's difficult, can be an important step in your own empowerment and it certainly is important in terms of his awareness. In this society, where men are supposed to be dominant and rape is sometimes regarded as something the woman always asks for, informing your rapist that what he did was a criminal act may prevent him from repeating his crime with someone else. You want to choose your place and your moment carefully. Make certain that you are not vulnerable to further attack – dominant males are aggressive, and being faced with criminal behavior may provoke him, to your detriment.

6. Work To Rebuild Your Self-Esteem And Self-Respect.

Whatever you do about your rapist, you are the most important person in this event. It is vitally important that you eliminate blame from yourself, and move yourself back to the person you were before the rape. You don't have to be naively trusting, but you don't have to question every man you date either. This book has gone into self-protecting behaviors at length. Start implementing them. Make certain that you don't drink alcohol when you're dating. Don't do drugs either. Protect everything you drink from date rape drugs. Date in packs. Have a friend watch your back while you watch her back. Don't go to his turf – stay out of parked cars, his car, his room, his apartment, or his office. If a date asks you why you're so skittish, tell him exactly why. Be powerful in establishing your boundaries. There is nothing that stops a man from abusing you faster than having his actions pointed out to him in front of other people.

7. Forgiveness

I said earlier that rape is an unforgivable crime – and it is. I also said you don't ever have to forgive your rapist – and you don't. What is important is to release yourself mentally and emotionally from the rapist so he doesn't continue to abuse you in your mind for the rest of your life. There is a fine line between not forgiving and being dominated by fear and anger that destroys your life. You have to get yourself beyond the violation – back to self-respect, back to getting on with the path of your life before you were violated.

There are rape victims who literally are still being raped in their minds fifteen and twenty years after the event. It destroys their lives. They are filled with such pain, rage and powerlessness that they cannot move on. Often this rage dominates them because they tried to do something about calling their rapist to task and were prevented by the authorities at the time. Those authorities might have been their family, their school, the church, the police, prosecutors, and even judges.

No matter what happened. No matter how infuriating. No matter how awful. No matter whether the rapist was punished or not, this is not about him, this is about you. You never have to forgive your rapist. You never have to forgive the people who prevented your justice. You don't even have to forget – not forgetting can be helpful in keeping you out of vulnerable situations in the future. This is about *self*-empowerment, *self*-esteem, *self*-love and not allowing a criminal to ruin your life. Whatever it takes, to get yourself back, do it. If it means putting the rapist in prison, do it. If it means seeking counseling, do it. If it means confronting the rapist, do it. If it means changing yourself into someone who can communicate your boundaries effectively, do it. Put the rape behind you and embrace life.

Also, if your rapist is still a man in your life, think long and hard about keeping him there. If that man doesn't accept responsibility for his actions, if it looks like you're facing a life of more of the same – take action. Being raped again and again is much worse than being raped and dealing with the problem right at the beginning. Cities and towns across America have safe houses for abused women and children. Chances are the behavior that led to the abuses these women suffered during their lives with these boyfriends or husbands was very evident before they got married and had children. Pay attention. Memorize the profile of the date rapist and see if it matches the man you are being abused by. Being put down, constantly controlled, or physically and mentally abused is not okay.

Being forced to "put out" because you're a girlfriend or a wife is not a healthy requirement in a relationship. If you're in one of these relationships, seek help. Get a support network. Get yourself strong and powerful. Make the most of your life. It is not necessary to stay in a bad relationship because you need someone to make you "whole." Make yourself whole before you get into the relationship. Treat yourself with respect, and demand it of your partner. Treat yourself the way you want others to treat you, so that you know what you want and can ask for it. Practice communicating with power. Don't be afraid of rejection – you don't want a man in your life who doesn't respect you as you respect yourself. And if someone insists on violating your boundaries as part of his "due" – move on. Believe it or not, there are many men in this world who will treat you well and with whom you do want to be in relationship.

Chapter 10
Help Others

This book helps me as much as it helps you. It's my attempt to right the wrong of my own rape by sharing information on how to avoid being raped or how to handle the rape after it happens. Becoming a Paramedic, helping people deal with being hurt or sick, was another great way for me to deal with what happened to me.

I encourage everyone to help their friends, to help strangers and to allow other people to help them, on whatever level. One of the things that has disappeared in our nuclear family way of life is that feeling of community that is actually vital to our well-being. Becoming part of a helping community is an important part of healing. Helping others is empowering and it builds self-esteem. Helping rape victims is a great way to talk to yourself by talking to others. I encourage you to become active in a helping community in whatever form you wish.

My Hypnosis Processes Are Designed to Help YOU.

Beyond Date Rape is a 22 minute process to help eliminate feelings of guilt and anger and recover from the rape so you can get back to your life.

Creating Boundaries is a 22 minute process designed to help you create mental boundaries that keep you safe, keep you listening to and acting on your intuition. It allows you to attract only self people into your space.

Getting Comfortable With Getting Naked is a *very* gently process to help you feel comfortable with getting naked if rape has made you nervous and you want to feel comfortable getting naked with a lover, or by yourself. It gives to permission to feel comfortable with your body.

These processes will soon be available on Amazon.com. They are currently available at www.joanmeijer/store.htm.

You've finished. Before you go…

<u>Tweet/share that you finished this book</u>

Rate this book.

Customers who bought this book also bought

*   Relentless: The Search for Typhoid Mary by Joan
Meijer
*   Provenance by Joan Meijer

Other books by this author

*   The President's Dirty Little Secret by John Russell
*   Accidental Consequences by John Russell

Coming Soon by this Author

*…The Bridge by John Russell

CPSIA information can be obtained at www.ICGtesting.com
Printed in the USA
LVOW10s1518050615

441363LV00020B/735/P